# THE COMPLETE ORGAN PLAYER
# SCOTTISH SONGBOOK

**Wise Publications**
London/New York/Sydney

Exclusive Distributors:
**Music Sales Limited**
8/9 Frith Street, London W1V 5TZ, England.
**Music Sales Pty, Limited**
120 Rothschild Avenue, Rosebery, NSW 2018, Australia.

This book © Copyright 1984 by
Wise Publications
UK ISBN 0.7119.0575.4
UK Order No. AM 37870

Designed by Howard Brown

Music Sales complete catalogue lists thousands of
titles and is free from your local music book shop,
or direct from Music Sales Limited.
Please send Cheque or Postal Order for £1.50 for postage to
Music Sales Limited, 8/9 Frith Street, London W1V 5TZ.

Printed in England by
Caligraving Limited, Thetford, Norfolk.

## CONTENTS

### SONGS

## SONG CATEGORY INDEX

# MULL OF KINTYRE

Words & Music: McCartney/Laine

O44 Pop Waltz    Jazz Organ O32

Registration No. ②
Suggested Drum Rhythm: **Waltz**

# ANNIE LAURIE

Traditional

Registration No. ⑤
Suggested drum rhythm: **Bossa nova**

# AN ERISKAY LOVE LILT

Words & Music: Kenneth MacLeod and Majory Kennedy-Fraser

Registration No. ①
Suggested Drum Rhythm: **Waltz**

# THE BLUEBELLS OF SCOTLAND

Traditional

Registration No. ⑧
Suggested Drum Rhythm: **Bossa Nova**

# THE SKYE BOAT SONG

Traditional

Registration No. ②
Suggested Drum Rhythm: **Waltz** (♩. = ♩.)

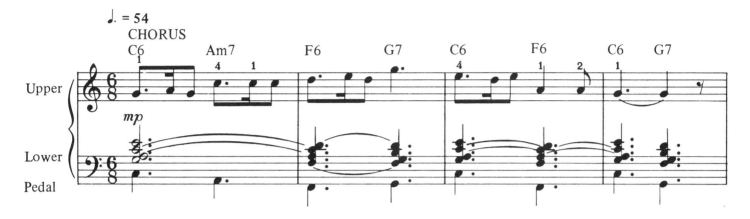

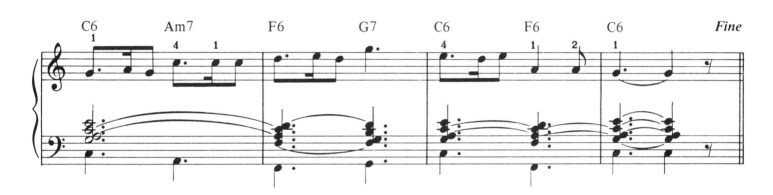

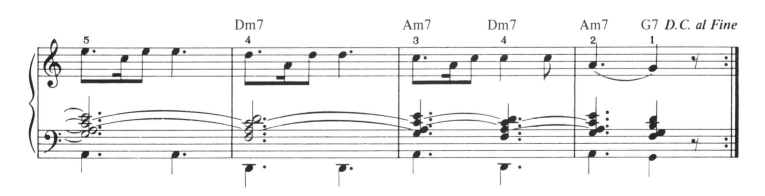

# YE BANKS AND BRAES

Traditional

Registration No. ① 
Suggested Drum Rhythm: **Waltz**

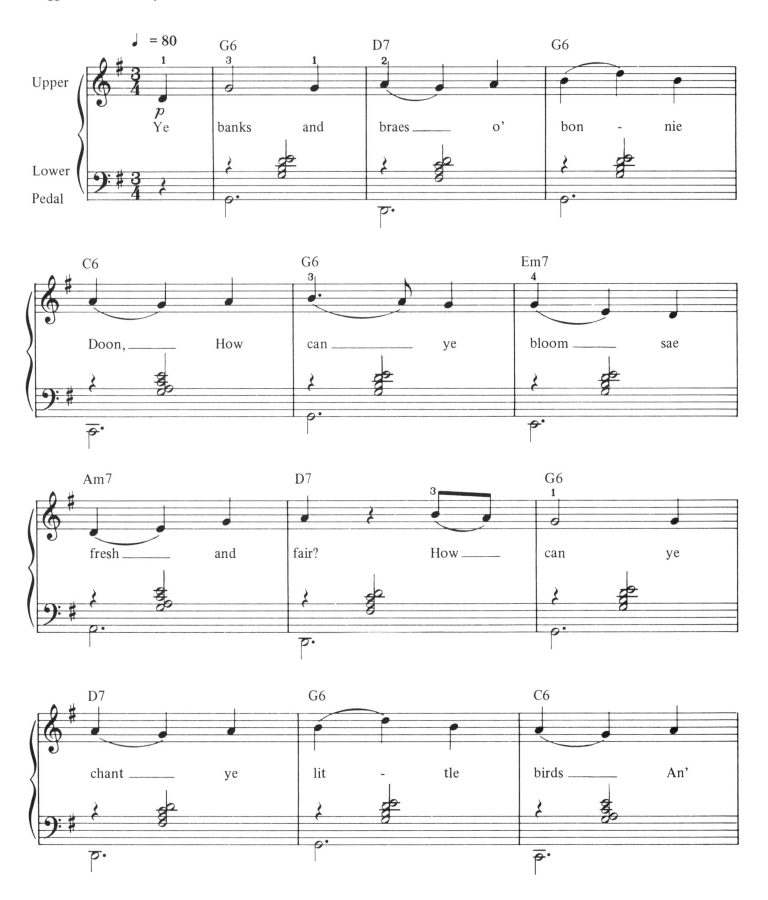

# THE DARK ISLAND

Words: David Silver
Music: Iain MacLachlan

Registration No. ⑦
Suggested Drum Rhythm: **Waltz**

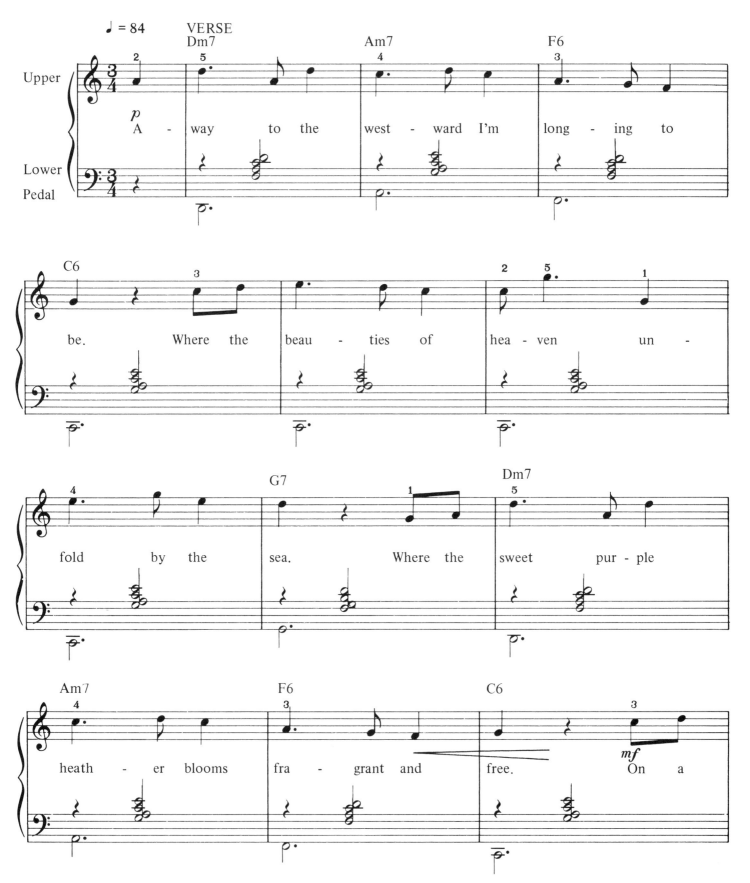

# LOCH LOMOND

Traditional

Registration No. ③
Suggested Drum rhythm: **Bossa nova** (changing to Swing at Chorus)

# COMIN' THROUGH THE RYE

Traditional

Registration No. ②
Suggested Drum Rhythm: **Bossa Nova**

# MY LOVE IS LIKE A RED, RED ROSE

Traditional

Registration No. ⑤
Suggested Drum Rhythm: **Bossa Nova**

# WILL YE NO COME BACK AGAIN

Traditional

Registration No. ⑧
Suggested Drum Rhythm: **Cha-Cha**

# SCOTLAND THE BRAVE

Traditional

('The song version of "Scotland The Brave" is © by James S. Kerr of Glasgow'.)

Registration No. ④
Suggested Drum Rhythm: **March** $\frac{2}{4}$ (or $\frac{4}{4}$)

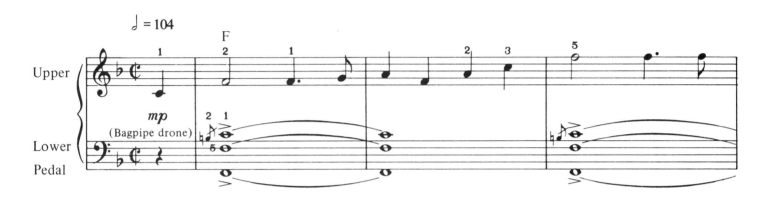

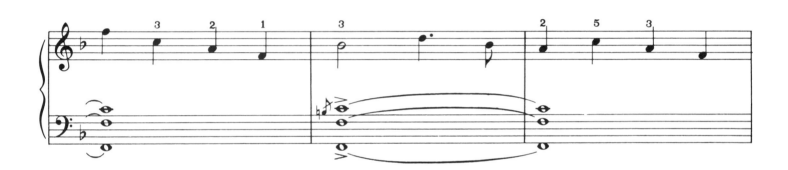

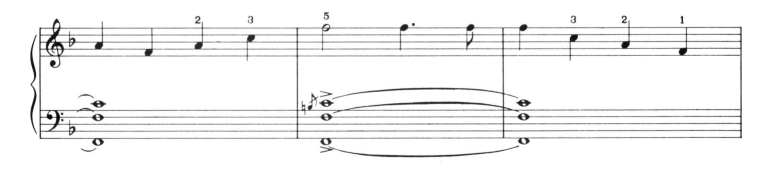

Vibrato: On

C7          F6

Dm7          C6          G7          C7     Vibrato: Off

F          mf          mp

19

# DOWN IN THE GLEN

Words & Music: Harry Gordon & Tommie Connor

Registration No. ③
Suggested Drum Rhythm: **Waltz**

# BONNY MARY OF ARGYLE

Traditional

Registration No. ⑧
Suggested Drum Rhythm: **Rock (or Bossa Nova)**

# MARCH FROM 'A LITTLE SUITE'

By: Trevor Duncan

Registration No. ⑥
Suggested Drum Rhythm: **March** $\frac{2}{4}$ (or $\frac{4}{4}$)

# SCOTCH ON THE ROCKS

By: W.J.G.Bates

Registration No. (7)
Suggested Drum Rhythm: **March** 2/4 (or 4/4)

# CHARLIE IS MY DARLIN'

Traditional

Registration No. ⑥
Suggested Drum Rhythm: **March** 6/8

2. As he cam' marchin' up the street,
   The pipes played loud and clear,
   And a' the folk cam' rinnin' out
   To meet the Chevalier.
        Oh! Charlie, etc.

3. Wi' Hieland bonnets on their heads,
   And claymores bright and clear;
   They cam' to fight for Scotland's right
   And the young Chevalier.
        Oh! Charlie, etc.

4. They've left their bonnie Hieland hills,
   Their wives and bairnies dear,
   To draw the sword for Scotland's lord,
   The young Chevalier.
        Oh! Charlie, etc.

# MY AIN FOLK

Words: Wilfred Mills
Music: Laura G. Lemon

Registration No. ⑤
Suggested Drum Rhythm: **Bossa Nova**

CHORUS

# THE ROAD TO THE ISLES

Words: Kenneth MacLeod
Music Arr: Patuffa Kennedy-Fraser

Registration No. ①
Suggested Drum Rhythm: **Swing**

2. It's by Sheil water, the track is to the west,
   By Aillort and by Morar to the sea,
   The cool cresses I am thinkin' o' for pluck,
   And bracken for a wink on Mother knee,
        Sure, by Tummel (etc.)

3. It's the blue Islands are pullin' me away,
   Their laughter puts the leap upon the lame,
   The blue Islands from the Skerries to the Lews,
   Wi' heather honey taste upon each name,
        Sure, by Tummel (etc.)

# THE GAY GORDONS

Traditional

Registration No. ⑥
Suggested Drum Rhythm: **March** 6/8

Upper: Add Piano

# THE BLUEBELL POLKA

Music: F. Stanley  Arranged by: Marion McClurg Words: Paddy Roberts

The Polka, a lively dance of Bohemian origin, first appeared about 1840. It is still danced today.

hand - some lad - die and he looked so good, I pro - mised that I'd meet him in the

Upper: Add Vibes

blue - bell wood. Half past se - ven by the old oak tree,

*mp*

I was wait - ing, an - ti - ci - pa - ting, what would hap - pen to a

Upper: Cut Vibes

girl like me, when he came a - long. Pick -in' a

blue - bell in the mer - ry month of May, and sud - den-ly I saw him

*mf*

39

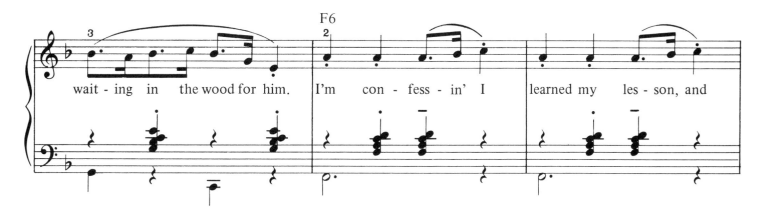

wait - ing in the wood for him. I'm con - fess - in' I learned my les - son, and

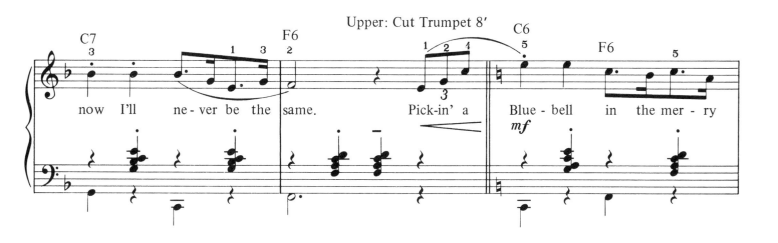

Upper: Cut Trumpet 8′

now I'll ne - ver be the same. Pick-in' a Blue - bell in the mer - ry

*mf*

month of May is some-thing I'll re-mem - ber when I'm old and grey, and if I

live to nine - ty two I know darn well, I ne - ver want to see an-oth - er Scots blue - bell.

# SCOTTISH JIG MEDLEY: 'THE CAMPBELLS ARE COMIN', 'BONNIE DUNDEE', 'WI' A HUNDRED PIPERS'

Traditional

Registration No. ⑥
Suggested Drum Rhythm: **March** 6/8

THE CAMPBELLS ARE COMIN'

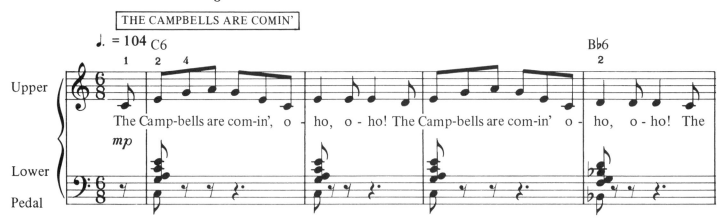

The Camp-bells are com-in', o - ho, o - ho! The Camp-bells are com-in' o - ho, o - ho! The

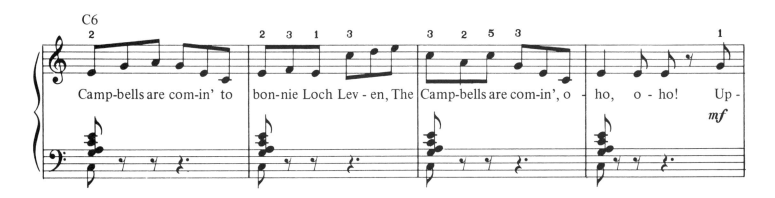

Camp-bells are com-in' to bon-nie Loch Lev - en, The Camp-bells are com-in', o - ho, o - ho! Up-

on the Lo-monds I lay, I lay __ Up - on the Lo-monds I lay, I lay. I

looked __ down to bon-nie Loch Lev - en, and saw __ three bon - nie perch-es play. To the

BONNIE DUNDEE

lords of con-ven-tion 'twas Cla-ver House spoke 'ere the King's crown go down there are

(bagpipe drone)

crowns to be broke, so each cav - a - lier who loves hon-our and me, let him

fol-low the bon-nets o' Bon-nie Dun-dee. Come fill up my cup come fill up my can, Come

Vibrato: On    G6    D7

sad - dle my hors-es, and call out my men.    Un-hook the West Port ___ and

G6    C6

let us gae free, for it's up wi' the bon-nets o' Bon-nie Dun-dee. Wi' a'

G6    C6    G6    D7    G6

43

WI' A HUNDRED PIPERS

hun - dred pi - pers an' a', an' a', a hun - dred pi - pers an'
a', an' a', we'll ___ up an' gie them a blaw, a blaw, a
hun - dred pi - pers an' a', and a'. Oh it's owre the Bor - der a -
wa', a - wa', it's ___ owre the Bor - der, a - 'wa', a - wa', we'll ___
on we'll march to Car - lisle ha', wi' its yetts, its cas - tle an' a' an' a'.

44

# AULD LANG SYNE

Traditional

Registration No. ⑦
Suggested Drum Rhythm: **Bossa Nova**

# CHORD CHARTS (For Left Hand)

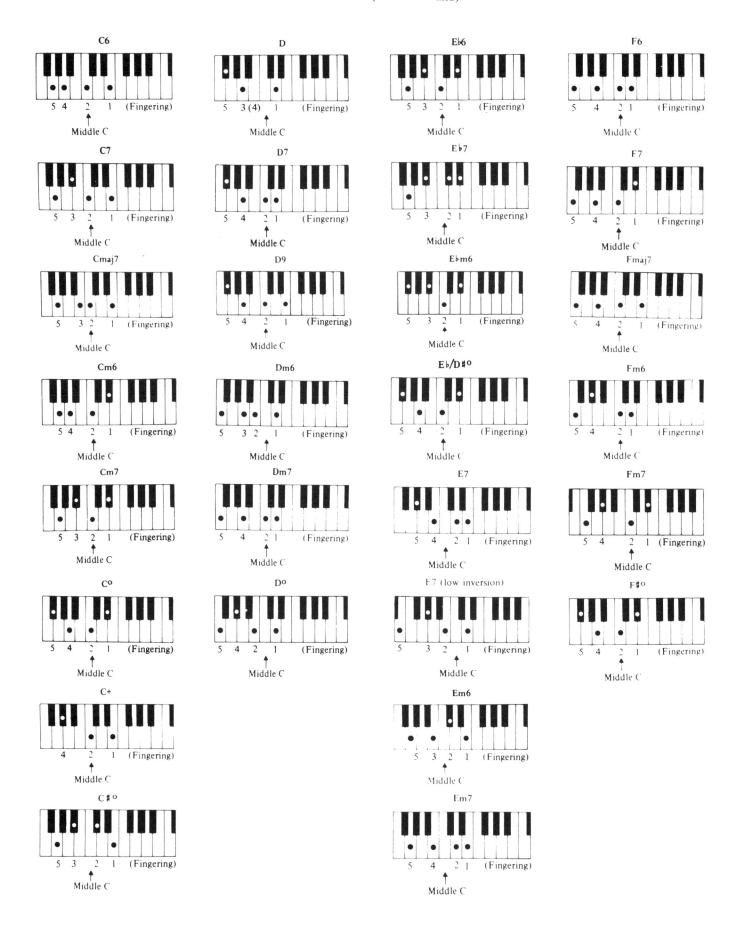

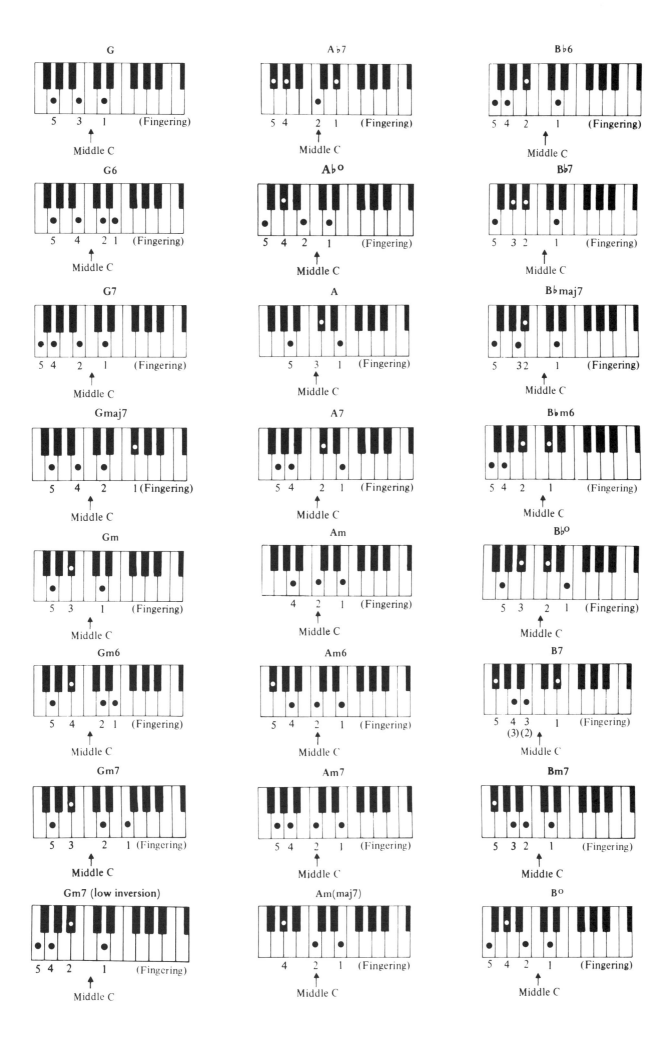

## REGISTRATION TABLE
### (For All Organs)

GENERAL ELECTRONIC ORGANS

(1) Upper: Clarinet 8'
Lower: Flute 8', String 8'
Pedal: 8'
Vibrato: On (or Off)

(2) Upper: Oboe (Reed) 8'
Lower: Flutes 8', 4'
Pedal: 8'
Vibrato: On

(3) Upper: Trumpet 8'
Lower: Diapason (or Flute) 8'
Pedal: 8'
Vibrato: Off. Leslie: Chorale

(4) Upper: Orchestral Strings (or Strings 8', 4')
Lower: Flutes 8', 4'
Pedal: 8'
Vibrato: On

(5) Upper: Flutes 16', 8', 4'
Lower: Flute 8', String 8'
Pedal: 16' + 8'
Vibrato: On (or Leslie: Tremolo)

(6) Upper: Flutes 8', 4', String 8'
Lower: Flutes 8', 4'
Pedal: 16' + 8'
Vibrato: Off. Leslie: Chorale (switching to Tremolo on appropriate verses)

(7) Upper: Flutes 16', 8', 4', Trumpet 8'
Lower: Flutes 8', 4', Horn 8'
Pedal: 16' + 8'
Vibrato: Off. Leslie: Chorale (switching to Tremolo on appropriate verses)

(8) Upper: Flutes 8', 4', Trombone 16', Trumpet 8'
Lower: Flutes 8', 4', Diapason 8'
Pedal: 16' + 8'
Vibrato: Off. Leslie: Chorale (switching to Tremolo on appropriate verses)

DRAWBAR ORGANS

(1) Upper: 00 7272 420
Lower: (00)7633 000(0)
Pedal: 4 – (2)
Vibrato: On (or Off)

(2) Upper: 00 5403 000
Lower: (00)4432 000(0)
Pedal: 4 – (2)
Vibrato: On

(3) Upper: 00 6888 852
Lower: (00)8754 220(0)
Pedal: 6 – (4)
Vibrato: Off. Leslie: Chorale

(4) Upper: 00 5675 542

Lower: (00)7604 000(0)
Pedal: 4 – (2)
Vibrato: On

(5) Upper: 70 7604 000
Lower: (00)5443 211(0)
Pedal: 5 – (3)
Vibrato: On (or Leslie: Tremolo)

(6) Upper: 00 8764 432
Lower: (00)5732 000(0)
Pedal: 4 – (3)
Vibrato: Off. Leslie: Chorale (switching to Tremolo on appropriate verses)

(7) Upper: 50 8655 304
Lower: (00)7633 455(0)
Pedal: 6 – (3)
Vibrato: Off. Leslie: Chorale (switching to Tremolo on appropriate verses)

(8) Upper: 83 8876 542

Lower: (00)6845 322(0)
Pedal: 6 – (4)
Vibrato: Off. Leslie: Chorale (switching to Tremolo on appropriate verses)

11/93 (16682)